THE BRENTWOOD
STATIONS OF THE CROSS

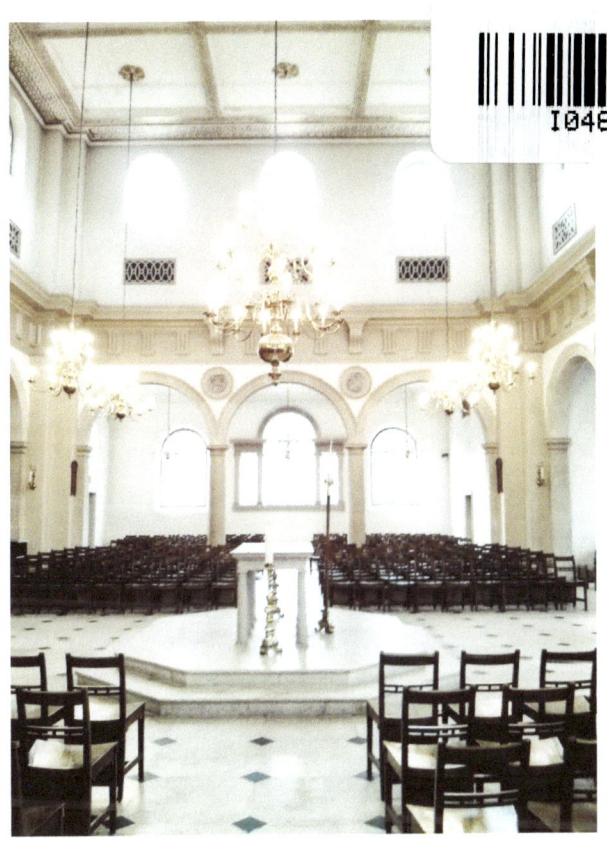

Fifteen Stations of the Cross by
fifteen contemporary painters

First shown at Brentwood Cathedral,
Ash Wednesday to Good Friday 2015

THE BRENTWOOD
STATIONS OF THE CROSS

Project devised by Fr. Martin Boland
Dean of Brentwood Cathedral

INTRODUCTION: FAITH IN PAINT

Simon Carter

Being a believer within a protestant non-conformist tradition does not make it easy to be a painter. Non-conformists have traditionally had a marked mistrust of imagery and a firm attachment to words. We like the idea of Jesus as the Word of God (John 1:1) but are less keen on him as the Image of God (Colossians 1:15). For a painter a mistrust of images is anathema.

In the early 1980's Ruth and I visited the Nolde Foundation in North Germany and saw Nolde's Life of Christ polyptych. I thought that to express my faith I would need to do something similar. There are moments and events in life that in retrospect assume unreasonable significance and it was the actual experience of visiting the Foundation that had a long after-life for me. We had cycled out of Denmark across flatlands of burnt stubble and drifting smoke. We were allowed to cross the border on a quiet back road as long as we promised to return the same day; the Foundation an isolated farmstead set among drainage dykes and a late summer flower garden.

In the studio I still have a large watercolour copy I made of the Nolde painting but it is the memory of being in that northern border landscape that also survives and it is the landscape that has continued to sublimate what I took to be expressions of faith. In recent years however, it has been pointed out that what I thought I had failed to express is still there, deeply embedded in the paintings. It appears that we cannot avoid who we are or what we think. Ideas in painting are not those of reasoned argument and explanation or of direct instruction. The painted surface is meaning in itself and leaves us dangerously free to think our own thoughts.

The passion of Jesus is not just a religious narrative; I would suggest that it is not even a religious narrative. It is a deeply human story, resonant and meaningful to all. Fifteen contemporary painters, some of faith and some of no faith, have taken on the challenge of considering anew the Stations of the Cross. I hope the resulting paintings ask questions of us, maybe give a few answers and, whether they lead us to contemplate divine salvation or questions of human suffering, they might provide a quiet space to consider again the story of Easter.

ESSAY: THE BRENTWOOD STATIONS OF THE CROSS

Fr. Martin Boland

The popular view is that religion and contemporary art hold each other in more or less tolerant disdain. For those who have religious beliefs, contemporary art, having given up on the pursuit of beauty and truth, is considered to be the decadent wing of secularism. Furthermore, many artists believe that religious iconography, having lost any cultural traction in a secular age, has retreated into the realm of the kitsch and the sentimental. In this project, I wanted to test these positions and see if it would be possible for religion and art to have a meaningful conversation.

Early on, I decided that if this dialogue was to take place then it would require a subject matter broad enough to embrace a variety of viewpoints. I wanted to fix the conversation in an unashamedly Christian context so that it did not float off into some spiritual stratosphere; and it seemed to me that the visual tradition of the Stations of the Cross would offer the range and imaginative scope for a mature exchange of ideas.

The Stations of the Cross is a devotional exercise peculiar to the Catholic tradition. It combines visual imagery with music, prayer and movement. The visual aspect – traditionally, fourteen painted or sculpted images that narrate the final moments of Christ's passion and death – can be seen lining the walls of every Catholic Church; and owe their origin to the via dolorosa found in Jerusalem. The word "Station" used in the sense of a halting place can be traced to a 15th century account of a pilgrimage to the Holy Land made by an Englishman called William Way. Over the centuries, this via sacra of the Holy Land was re-imagined in liturgical form in an effort to respond to the spiritual needs of people for every place and every time.

The images of the Stations of the Cross seek to confront the viewer both emotionally, morally and spiritually. They exist to inspire prayer and to lead the Christian believer through the vast mysterium passionis toward the mysterium paschale. Thus, the beauty of redemption is revealed to those who contemplate these images of brutality and suffering, as they progress slowly, in prayer, from one Station to the next.

Settings for conversations can be crucially important. I considered using neutral environments such as halls, crypts and gallery spaces, but on reflection I felt they were unlikely to stimulate truly creative responses. It seemed, therefore, that the obvious setting would be Brentwood Cathedral itself, a church where for the last six years I have been the Dean. Designed by Quinlan Terry in his characteristic neo-Palladian style, the Cathedral would provide a light and airy space in which to show the work. At the same time, as a place of prayer and worship, it would provide an extra dimension to any discussion. Art in this environment exists as an aid to the contemplation of invisible, supernatural realities. The Cathedral already had its own contemporary Stations created by the sculptor, Raphael Maklouf, best known perhaps for designing the image of the Queen on our coinage; but what kind of conversation would these two very different sets of Stations initiate?

So, I had my subject and my setting, and all I needed now was to find the right occasion for the conversation to take place. Liturgical time seemed to answer that need, and I decided that the dialogue would run throughout Lent. This period ".... the time of tension between dying and birth," as T.S.Eliot puts it in his poem, Ash Wednesday, would thus provide a perfect occasion to meet and to speak to each other.

I knew I didn't want installations or video pieces, for they risked making any conversation glib or ironic. I didn't want sculptures because they wouldn't be easy to show. My innate instinct was more conservative, and I wanted contemporary painters who would be up to the challenge of having a mature discourse with people of faith. I, therefore, needed fourteen painters, one for each Station.

Clearly, a quick consultation of the Yellow Pages or a search on Google would not allow me to find them. So, I arranged to meet the artist, Robert Priseman, for lunch at the National Gallery; and towards the end of our meal, I ambushed him with the question, "Can you find me fourteen painters to create a new Stations of the Cross for Brentwood?" He took a reflective sip of his cappuccino and replied, "Of course, leave it to me."

Within forty-eight hours, I had not fourteen, but fifteen of the finest living British painters signed up for the project, artists who were critically respected and who had pieces in both major public and private collections. Drawn from across the country, the artists included those with a degree of religious belief and those with none. The conversation was about to get started.

Each artist was given the title of a different Station together with an identical blank twelve inch square aluminium panel. The artists would be completely free to respond to their allocated subject in whatever way they chose. Of course, I knew this might be something of a risk; and there was clearly a danger of ending up with fourteen or fifteen images that bore little or no relationship to each other. The other potential hazard was that the artists might use their paintings for ideological purposes seeking to ridicule belief. But they didn't, and the resulting works exhibited a respect for the subject and a seriousness of purpose that brought the individual pieces together as *The Brentwood Stations of the Cross.*

The first Station, Jesus is condemned to death, by David Ainley introduces many of the concerns of contemporary art. He eschews pious illustration in favour of an image that is saturated with multivalent meanings. Ainley has created a chalky-white picture plane etched with vertical grooves. A simple cross cut from the support has been slotted, rather like a jigsaw piece, back into the painting. The monochrome surface could be thought of as symbolising the blank mental response of the condemned Jesus. The Cross, cut out of the blankness, is thus a momentary recognition of his fate. Below the surface image, traces of colour are visible, which were Ainley's original colour analysis of The Arrest of Christ by Fra Angelico. His Cross could be either a kiss or a multiplication sign, or even possibly the X factor of someone special. Alternatively, it could perhaps be 'X marks the spot', an indication that highlights something that is wrong or needs to be eliminated. Ainley allows these associations to build up a picture of Christ.

The sign of the Cross appears as a visual leitmotif in many of the Stations. Sometimes it acts as a strong geometric form that can bear the weight of abstract ideas as in Pen Dalton's Jesus falls the Second Time, where the Cross fixes an amorphous wave of biological matter; or in Susan Gunn's Jesus is taken down from the Cross, where geometry scythes a distressed picture plane. In other works, the Cross becomes a theological hieroglyph needing to be deciphered. Ruth Philo's tenth Station, Jesus is stripped of his garments, dissolves the image back to almost nothing, and we are left with a pink fleshy hue etched with scratch marks, including a central, spidery cross. This is a death of a thousand nicks and cuts, a violence that is at once both subtle and brutal. While working on this Station the artist was inspired by a comment found in Dietrich Bonhoeffer's Letters and Papers in Prison, "Even in this place we ought to live as if we had no wishes and no future and just be our true selves."

Other artists have decided to focus on a physical detail. Robert Priseman's Jesus is nailed to the Cross isolates two iron nails. Using recent archaeological evidence, Priseman paints them to the actual size and dimensions of nails found in crucified bodies. Without resorting to a cheap torture porn image, this Station's understated account of the physical sadism endured by Christ moves the viewer to compassion. The London based artist, Matthew Krishanu hones in on the textile used by Veronica to wipe the face of Jesus. Veronica, whose name means true icon, is the proto image-maker of Christ. She holds in her hands a length of cotton calico, a surface historically favoured by painters. In this image, Krishanu seems to highlight the moment of uncertainty experienced by any artist as he or she approaches Christ in an effort to capture his image. For Gideon Pain in Jesus meets his Mother, the detail of Mary and Jesus reaching out for each other, their fingers straining to make contact, vividly articulates the cruelty and heartbreak of the moment.

A memory or psychological state has also provided a source of inspiration. For example, Marguerite Horner's Station, Jesus dies on the Cross, was, she says, "inspired by an experience I had in Venice many years ago when I was going through a particularly difficult time and so, in a state of near desperation, I went into a church and prayed for help...I was laying the burden of my suffering at the foot of the Cross, hence the fiery red flowers."

Similarly, Susie Hamilton's Jesus meets the women of Jerusalem, distills the intensity of grief experienced by the women, with a looseness of brush stroke that is capable of holding the emotional content of their encounter with Christ.

Ideas about location and place occur in the works of both Freya Purdue, Jesus carries his cross, and Linda Ingham, Jesus falls for the first time. Purdue has created a contemporary labyrinth, a single route ornamented with gem-like punctuation symbolising each Station. The image acts as a spiritual route-map, helping the viewer to find his way through the trauma of Christ's suffering.

Linda Ingham, by contrast, imagines Jesus's fall through a grille of thorns. In her landscape, the foreground is presented as jagged and forbidding, while in the distance lie warmer, less threatening plains. At every fall, Ingham reminds us, is the ever-powerful human desire to lift oneself up and continue the journey. In theological terms, this is seen as Christ courageously pushing onwards through his sufferings and finally embracing Calvary.

Artists who make no claim to a personal faith have inevitably approached their particular Station through the lens of their own absence of religious conviction. Andrew Crane uses plaster, kindling and oil paint to sculpt a response to his title, Simon of Cyrene helps Jesus carry the Cross. There is an earthiness about his image that reminds us of how the smallest act of kindness grounds our humanity. Crane has broken a piece of kindling wood and then reassembled it on the aluminium plane in the form of a Cross. For him this resonates with the words of Jesus quoted in the apocryphal Gospel of Thomas, "Split a piece of wood; I am there."

David Sullivan, an avowed humanist, sees in his Station, Jesus falls for the third time, universal resonances. "Falling Christ, forced to the ground under the weight of his Cross is a powerful metaphor for humanity's descent towards despair," he says. The resulting abstract image defies easy interpretation and weighs heavy on the mind of the viewer.

Both the presence and the absence of the divine are recurring motifs in these works. Alex Hanna finds in a discarded, empty pill packet a symbol that communicates the event of Jesus being laid in the tomb. At one level, this is an image of an object that has been used and discarded, and is no longer considered of value. However, Hanna invites us to look beyond the utilitarian and to meditate on the beauty and life-giving power of that thing or person. In Simon Carter's fifteenth Station of the Cross, Jesus rises from the dead, a faceless figure wearing a floppy gardener's hat stands square on to us. We know it is meant to be Jesus, but we inevitably struggle to recognise him. In this failure, we experience something of the same uncertainty of those disciples who first encountered the risen Christ.

The artists who created the Brentwood Stations of the Cross have approached this challenge with the same creative openness and intellectual rigour which they would have applied to any other subject; and this project has shown not only that art and faith can find creative ways to talk to one other, but that they have a real moral imperative so to do.

The question now is can the believers who encounter these images during the season of Lent manage to do the same?

THE STATIONS OF THE CROSS

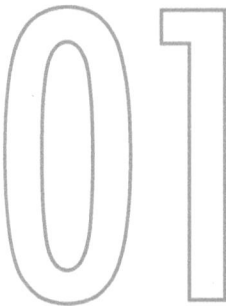

JESUS IS CONDEMNED TO DEATH

David Ainley

Conspicuously eschewing the figurative narrative traditionally adopted in paintings of the Stations of the Cross this ostensibly simple image invites viewers to engage with the Passion on several levels, emotional, intellectual and spiritual.

Distinct from a Latin cross, the best-known symbol of Christianity related to the Crucifixion, X has other connotations: a kiss, the identification of an individual, a location, an indescribable quality that makes someone special, an unknown quantity and, significantly in this Station, a condemnation, an elimination. Paradoxes are embodied in this form (Judas' kiss in the betrayal, a death sentence but also a symbol of love).

The work is made of multiple layers of monochrome, each one incised with numerous horizontal lines revealing something of the underpainting before repetition with different colours. The source of the colours was an analysis of *The Arrest of Christ* (c.1450) by Fra Angelico. The cross is cut out of the support and reinserted.

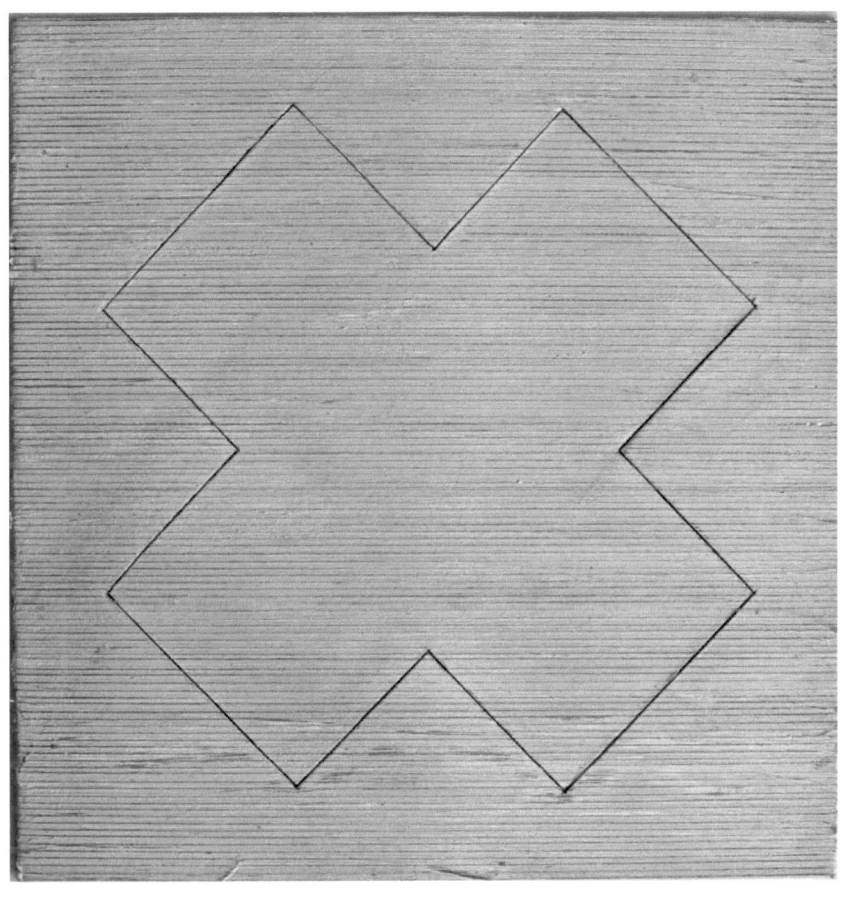

Acrylic and oil on cut-through aluminium. 30 x 30cm

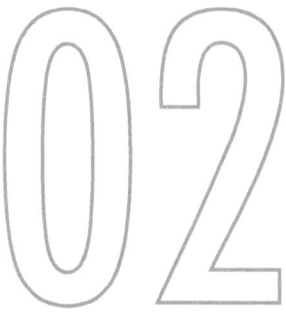

JESUS CARRIES HIS CROSS

Freya Purdue

Following the condemnation to death of Jesus, his journey begins and before him lie the inevitable events that unfold and lead to his resurrection symbolized in my painting as the labyrinth. It is the symbolic journey of the human Soul and has been represented using a labyrinth in both ancient and modern traditions including Christianity.

The adoption of the labyrinth by the Christian faith began during the Roman period. The first known pavement labyrinth with obvious Christian context is found in a basilica in Algeria during the 4th century. At first the labyrinth appeared mainly in manuscripts, but during the 12th century they began to appear in the cathedrals of Italy and during the 13th century spread to France where many fine examples were constructed. One of the most famous is the Labyrinth in the Cathedral of Chartres. The labyrinth is traditionally walked by pilgrims as a spiritual practice and today modern pilgrims still walk it as a meditation of the stations of the cross at Easter time.

2014 *@PaintBritain,* Ipswich Art School Gallery
2014 *Contemporary British Painting,* Huddersfield Art Gallery
2014 *Shrine Paintings,* Marylebone Church Crypt Gallery, London
2014 *Freya Purdue Paintings 2,* Letchworth Arts Centre
2014 *Action: Abstract Painting,* Swindon Museum & Art Gallery
2013 *Scope,* Miami Beach, International Contemporary Art Show

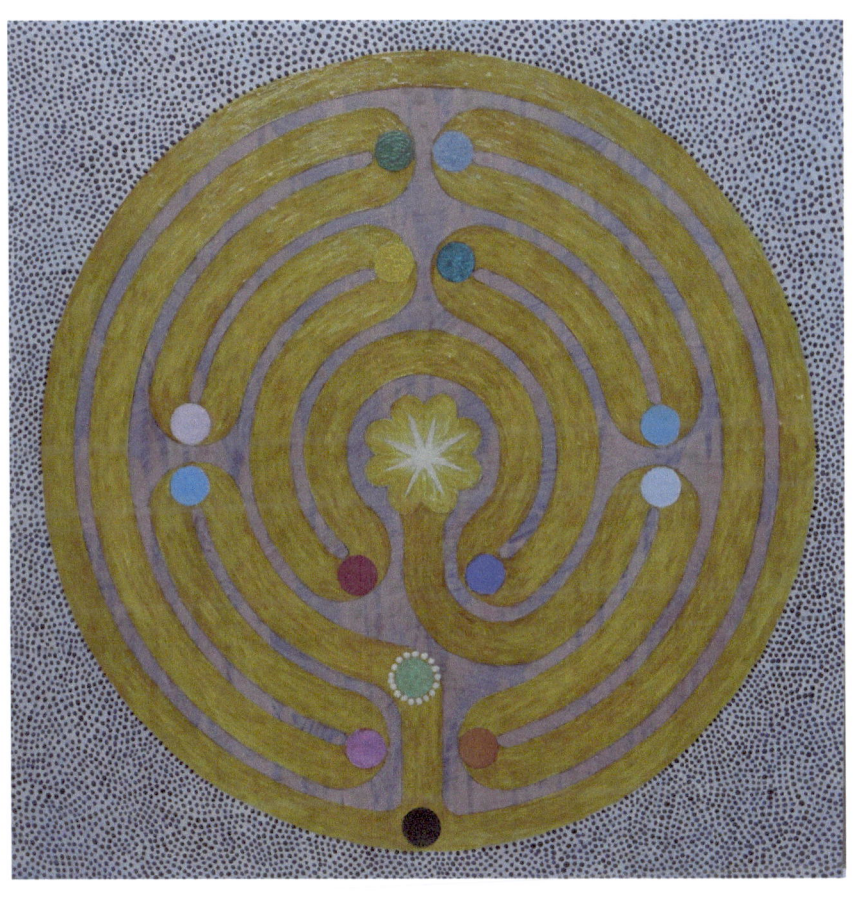

Oil on aluminium. 30 x 30cm

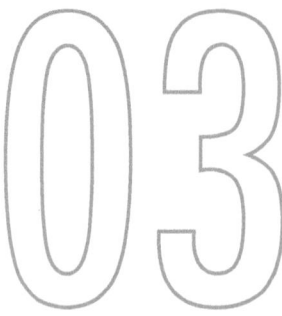

JESUS FALLS THE FIRST TIME

Linda Ingham

Begun during early autumn when the cycle of nature declines towards a temporary death, this piece follows my habit of acknowledging the nature of the passage of time as a recurring aspect of my work.

The representation of an autumnal landscape of a woodland interior and the surrounding Wolds has been my way into metaphor attempting to express the tenacious determination of human nature. The vivid shadow-stain of dying Pink Campions reminds me of the scarlet robe the stripped Christ was forced to wear by the soldiers prior to crucifixion (Matthew 27:1),here viewed through a curtain of thorns. To raise and proceed with dignity after a fall calls upon one's inner spirit coupled with the inevitability of what has to be, despite the everyday – or extraordinary – obstacles we may find in our path.

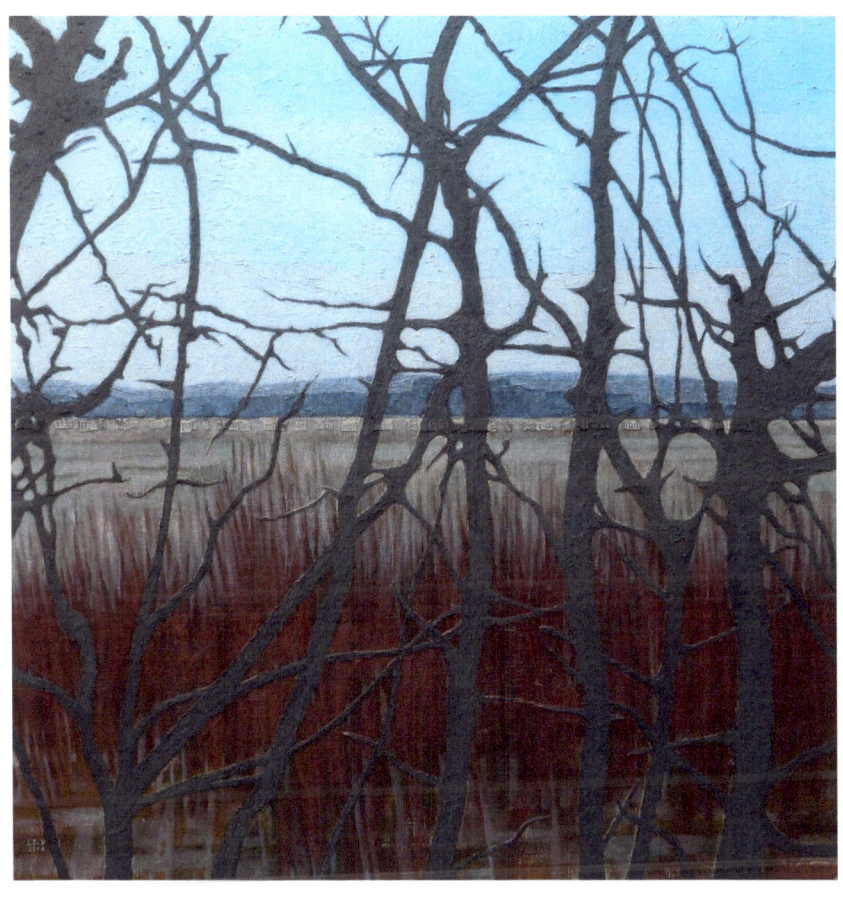

Oil on aluminium. 30 x 30cm

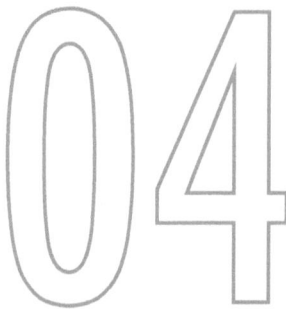

JESUS MEETS HIS MOTHER

Gideon Pain

I must confess that after the initial excitement of being asked to participate in this project I found the actual process of making the painting a daunting one. The pain of a mother at the loss of a child is a sadly familiar story, played out nightly on news programmes and media feeds. Be it by accident, cataclysm or at the hands of others, the images of grief, helplessness and regret never fail to move. The meeting in the crucifixion story is not a private one but instead played out in the hatred, craziness and brutality of a mob. This makes for a complex and confusing narrative. I used the idea of a last touch as a point of focus in this turmoil. This simple connection of hands is as much about Mary's desire to protect her child as it is her resignation and sacrifice at letting him go, for the greater good of all.

2014   *43 British Painters,* The Crypt, Marylebone, London
2014   *@PaintBritain,* Ipswich Art School Gallery
2014   *Contemporary British Painting,* Huddersfield Art Gallery
2014   *About Face,* Swindon Museum and Art Gallery
2014   *A Day at the Beach,* Waterbeach, Cambridge
2013   *Moving On,* Cambridge Art Salon

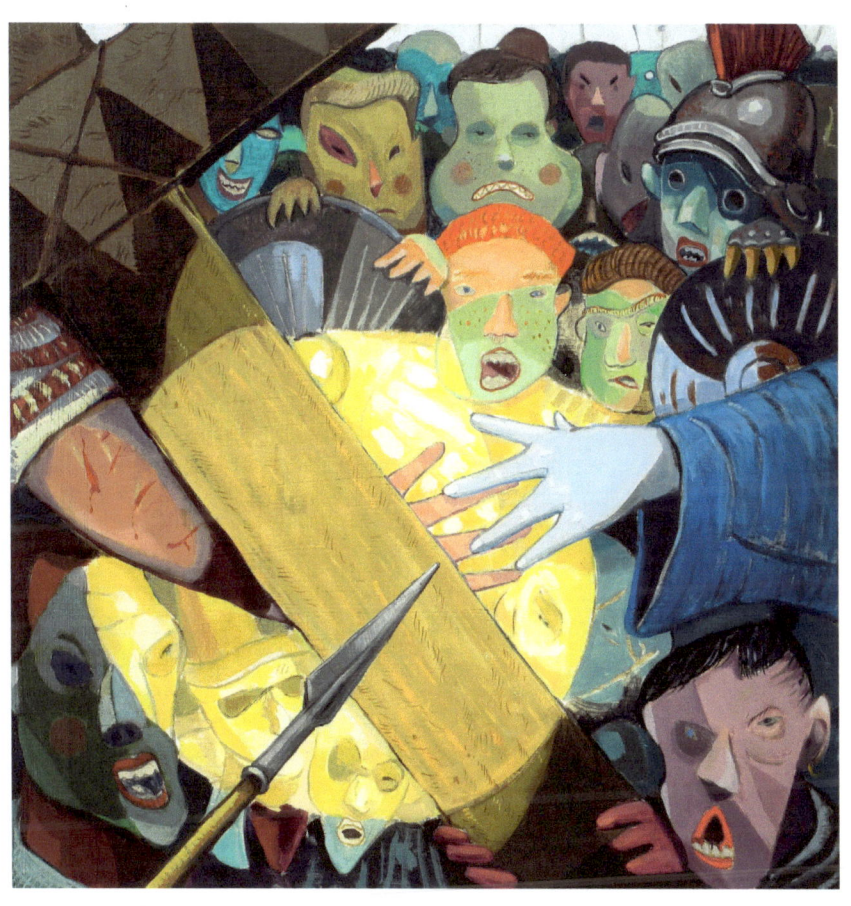

Oil on aluminium. 30 x 30cm

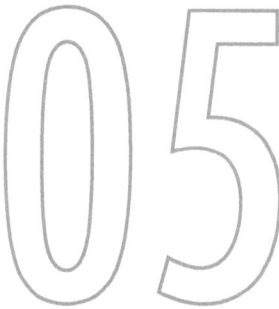

SIMON OF CYRENE HELPS JESUS CARRY THE CROSS

Andrew Crane

For me, this piece is all about physicality, the frailty and impermanence of the human body and the joy of giving oneself in an act of kindness.

The cross is composed of kindling sticks...broken by hand. Words spoken by Jesus from the beautiful Gospel of Thomas sprang to mind, *Split a piece of wood; I am there.* The numbers relate to ancient numerology: 1271 = Stavros (The Cross); 1480 = Jesus Christ. The cross itself, for me, represents the marriage of 'heaven and earth' - the horizontal axis being 'the physical' and the vertical, 'the spiritual'. Of course, it is only in the mind where this duality occurs and Christ pointed to this when he said, *If two make peace with each other in a single house, they will say to the mountain, 'Move from here!' and it will move.*

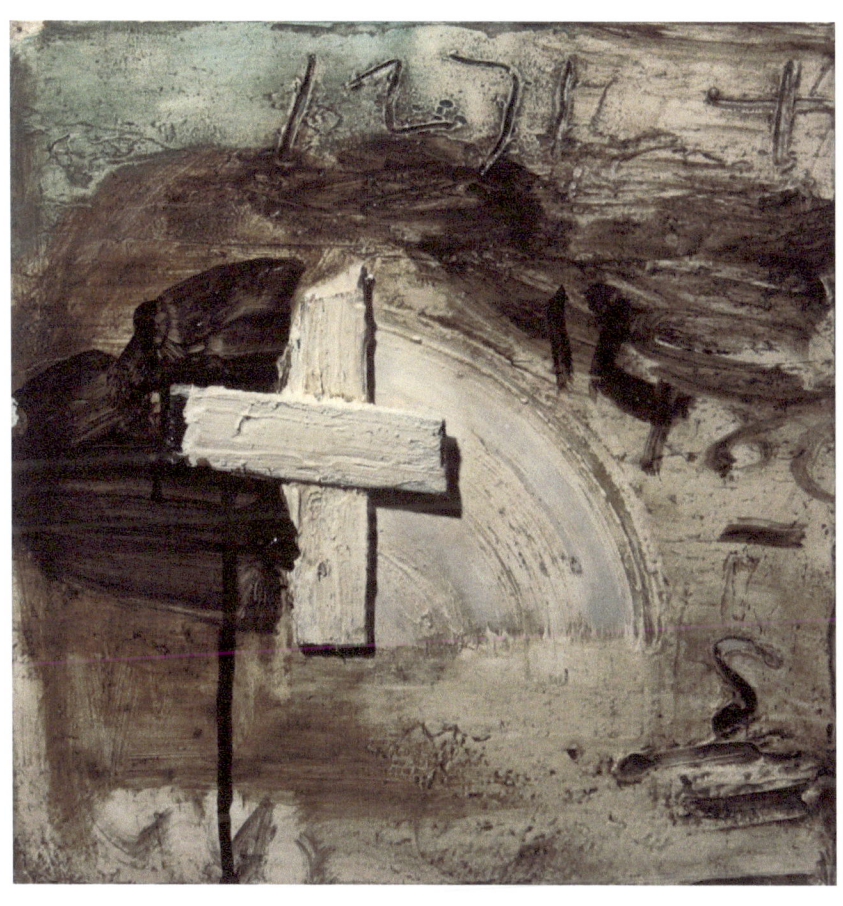

Plaster, kindling and oil on aluminium. 30 x 30cm

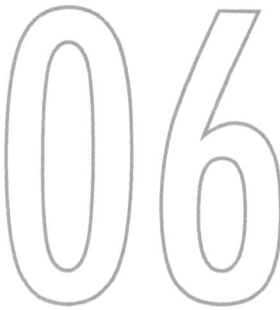

VERONICA WIPES THE FACE OF JESUS

Matthew Krishanu

My focus for the painting is Veronica herself.

The veil she holds is cotton calico, a painting surface. Veronica was the creator of the first image of Christ.

The cloth is blank – the work depicts Veronica in the moment before wiping Jesus' face.

2014   *The Griffin Art Prize,* Griffin Gallery, London
2014   *In the City,* Lion & Lamb, London
2014   *Home,* Dean Clough, Halifax
2014   *Another Country,* The Nunnery, London
2013   *Marmite Prize for Painting* (UK tour)

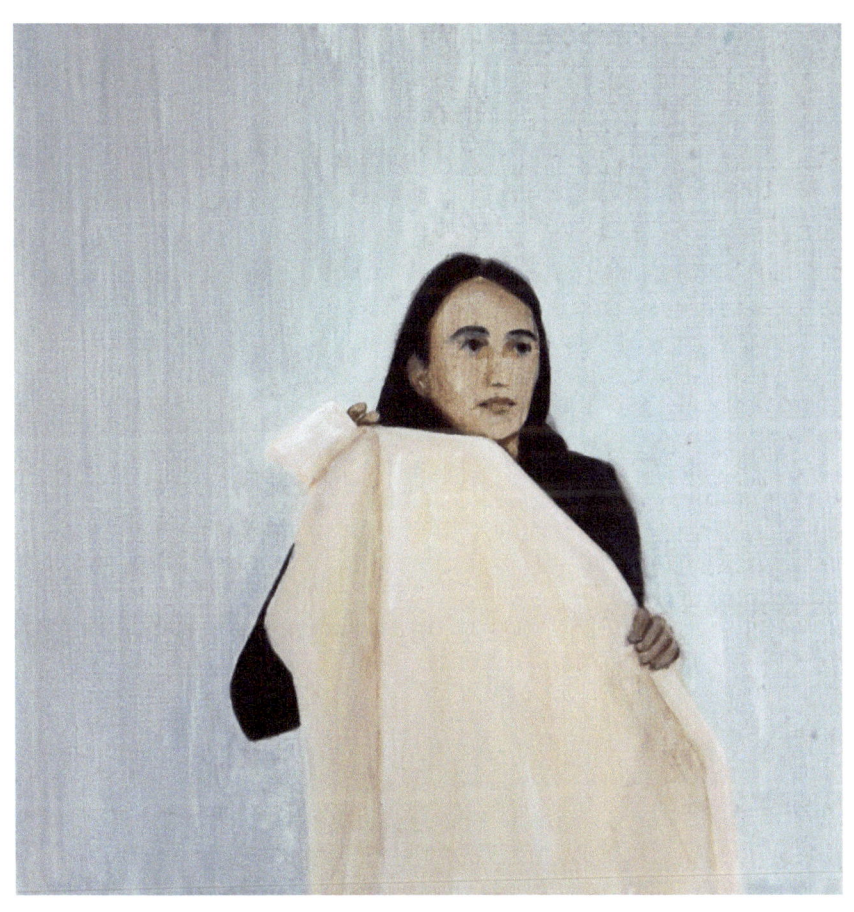

Acrylic on aluminium. 30 x 30cm

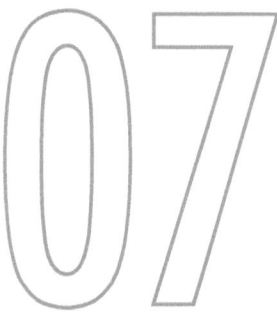

JESUS FALLS THE SECOND TIME

Pen Dalton

My paintings are usually abstract: I rely on form - colour, line, techniques of paint application - to suggest meaning. Realistic faces must be painted in terms of gender, age and race so I was reluctant to use these pictorial conventions for Jesus. I can assume everyone knows he was a young man, and eliminating facial detail makes it easier for others – women, the old, the racially different - to identify with painterly ambiguity. I also reduced Jesus' body to a series of abstract brushstrokes. The agitation of the paint, the disturbed skin of the impasto, the bleeding of separate colours into each other suggest, but do not dictate, the imagining of suffering. Painted lines are dragged down in motions that imitate falling but then rise again in animated loops and swirls analogous to what I understand as the narrative message of the seventh station: that this fall is followed by a subsequent and ultimate rise again.

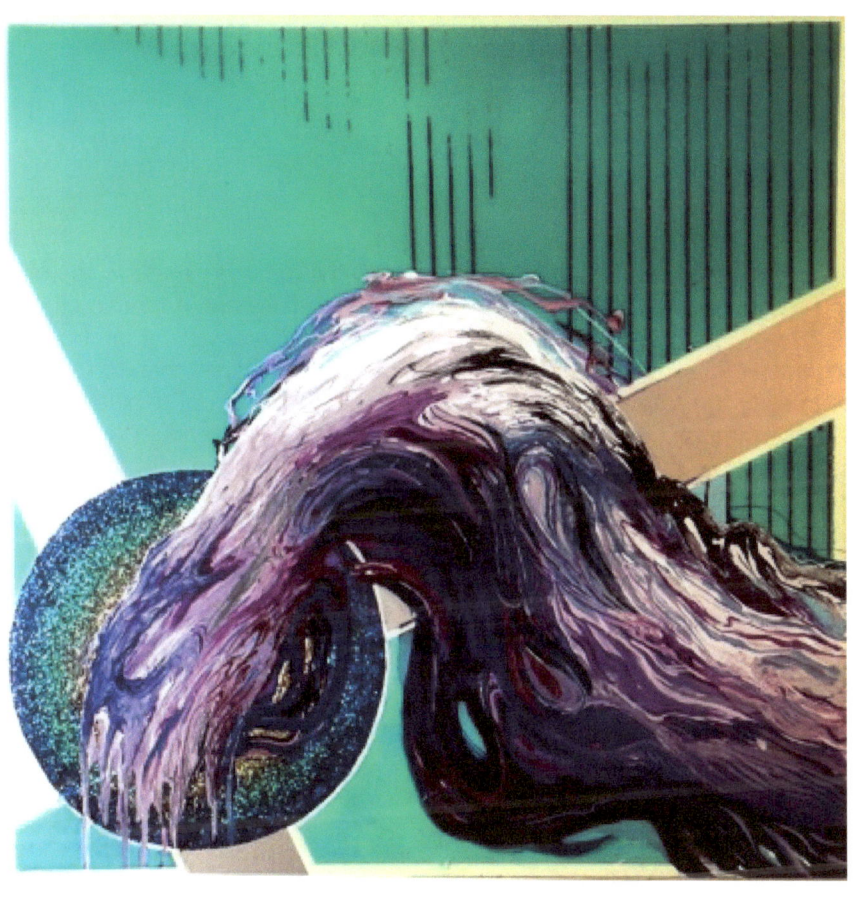

Acrylic on aluminium. 30 x 30cm

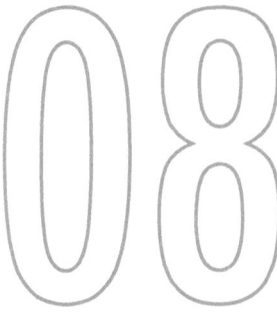

JESUS MEETS THE WOMEN OF JERUSALEM

Susie Hamilton

Jesus talks to the weeping women about all the disasters that are to come and so my figures are dressed anachronistically. They are in Islamic clothes as if they are in modern-day Syria or Iraq and are victims of violence occurring in our own time. Behind them are twisted shapes that could either be trees or the structures of demolished buildings. I have not depicted Jesus but I have made the lamenting woman in the yellow garments look luminous as if reflecting his light. Through the use of light, associated with the spiritual in all religious traditions, there is the suggestion of salvation or the presence of the holy in the middle of this scene of despair.

2014   *John Moore's Painting Prize,* Walker Art Gallery, Liverpool
2014   *The Threadneedle Prize,* Mall Galleries, London
2014   Summer Exhibition, Royal Academy, London
2014   *Derwent Art Prize,* Mall Galleries, London
2014   Three person show, Paul Stopler, London
2014   International Print Biennale, Hatton Gallery, Newcastle

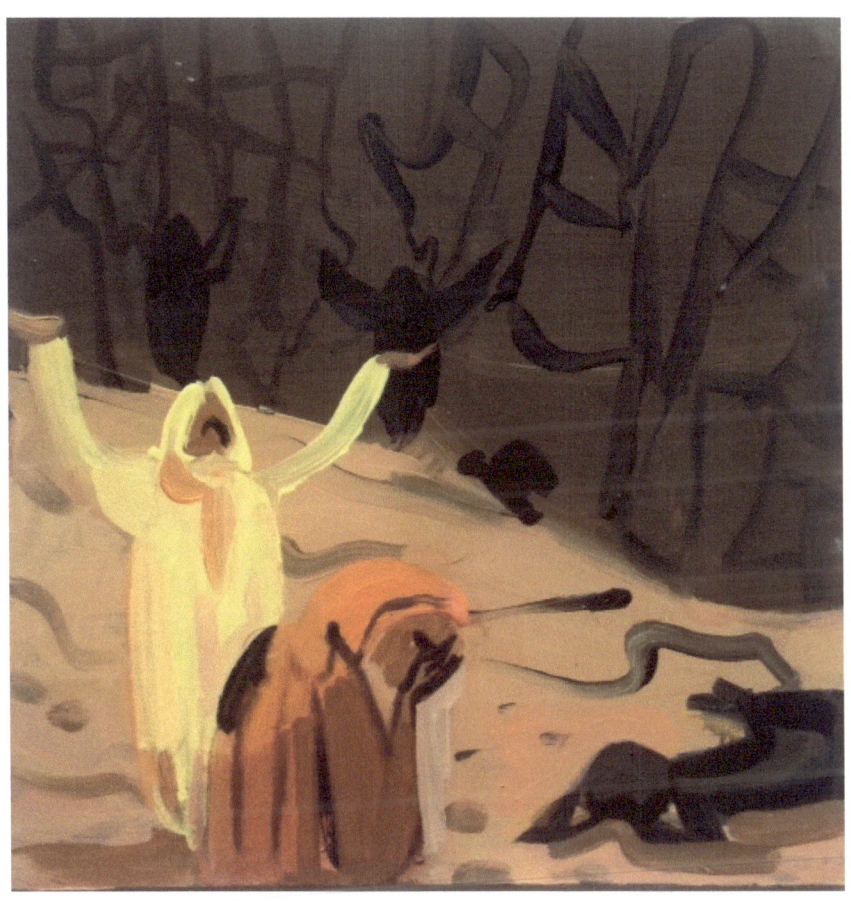

Acrylic on aluminium. 30 x 30cm

JESUS FALLS THE THIRD TIME

David Sullivan
inspired by a design from Charles Rennie Mackintosh

The first and last problem in approaching the making of work is always the same, to discover the set of circumstances, the emergent phenomena, that coalesce to make for strong and coherent painting. The first attempt at Station 9 collapsed into an overly anguished self portrait, and as such had to be abandoned. Simultaneously, the source for the final work found its way to my studio, without searching for it as if it had been left there deliberately.

Whilst I judge myself a Humanist and fully detached from religion, I repeatedly return to themes of a contemporary 'human condition'. Not only subjects that impart our collective suffering, but also to those aspects of life which allow for measures of redemption, and optimism for lived experience. Falling Christ, forced to the ground under the weight of his cross is a powerful metaphor for humanity's descent toward despair. With faith however, we can also perhaps find the courage and the strength to persevere.

2014   *@PaintBritain,* Ipswich Art School Gallery
2014   *Contemporary British Painting,* Huddersfield Art Gallery
2014   *Towards a new Socio-Painting,* Transition Gallery, London
2012   *Summer Exhibition,* Royal Academy,London
2010   *400 Women,* Shoreditch Town Hall, London
2010   *Threadneedle Prize,* Mall Galleries, London

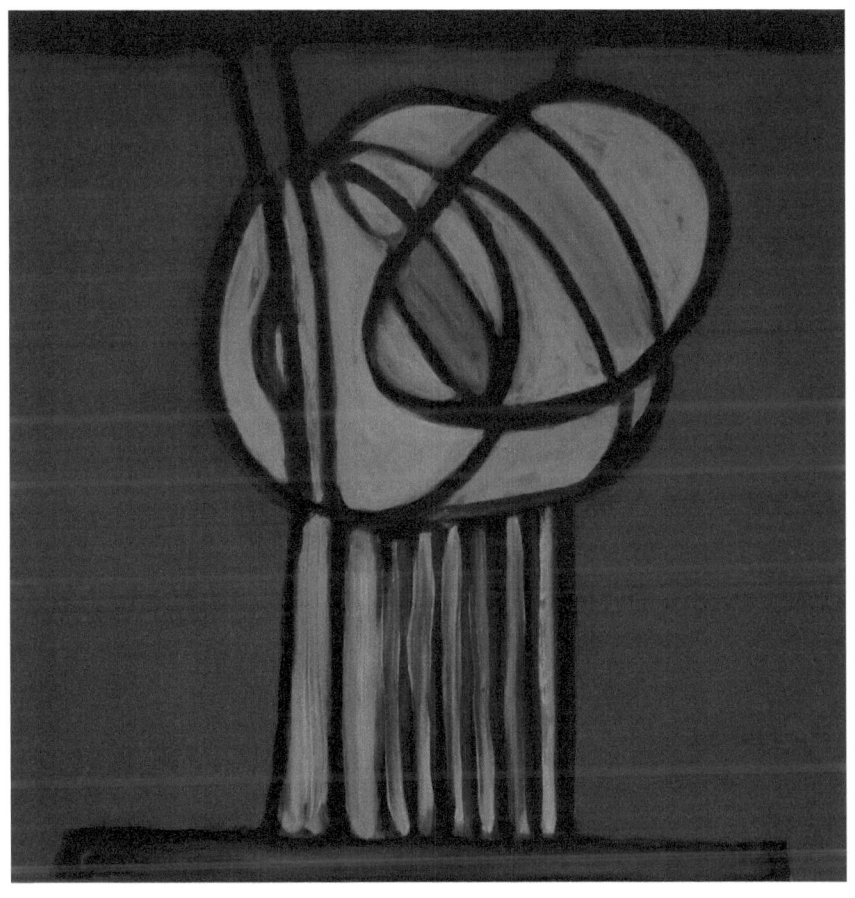

Oil on aluminium. 30 x 30cm

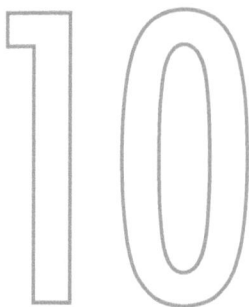

JESUS IS STRIPPED BARE OF HIS GARMENTS

Ruth Philo

My paintings are concerned with abstract qualities of surface, mark and colour and are gradually becoming more minimal. The subject of Christ stripped bare challenged me to pare down further. I am interested in paintings as contemplative pieces, where the viewer can bring their own feelings and interpretation to bear. A small painting like this is intended to work face to face as a kind of intimate abstraction. Whilst painting I thought considerably about the concept of this station of the cross and also read some of Dietrich Bonhoeffer's diary excerpts and letters from prison, which evoke for me what the piece is about. The stripping bare, 'Even in this place we ought to live as if we had no wishes and no future and just be our true selves'.

Dietrich Bonhoeffer 'Letters & Papers from Prison'

2014   *@PaintBritain*, Ipswich Art School Gallery
2014   *Contemporary British Painting*, Huddersfield Art Gallery
2014   *Another Shade of Green*, The Benham Gallery, Colchester
2014   Cley 14 A Creative Conversation, Cley next the Sea
2014   ART Converters! Studio 1.1, Redchurch Street, London
2013   *Beyond the Façade*, Blickling Hall, Norfolk

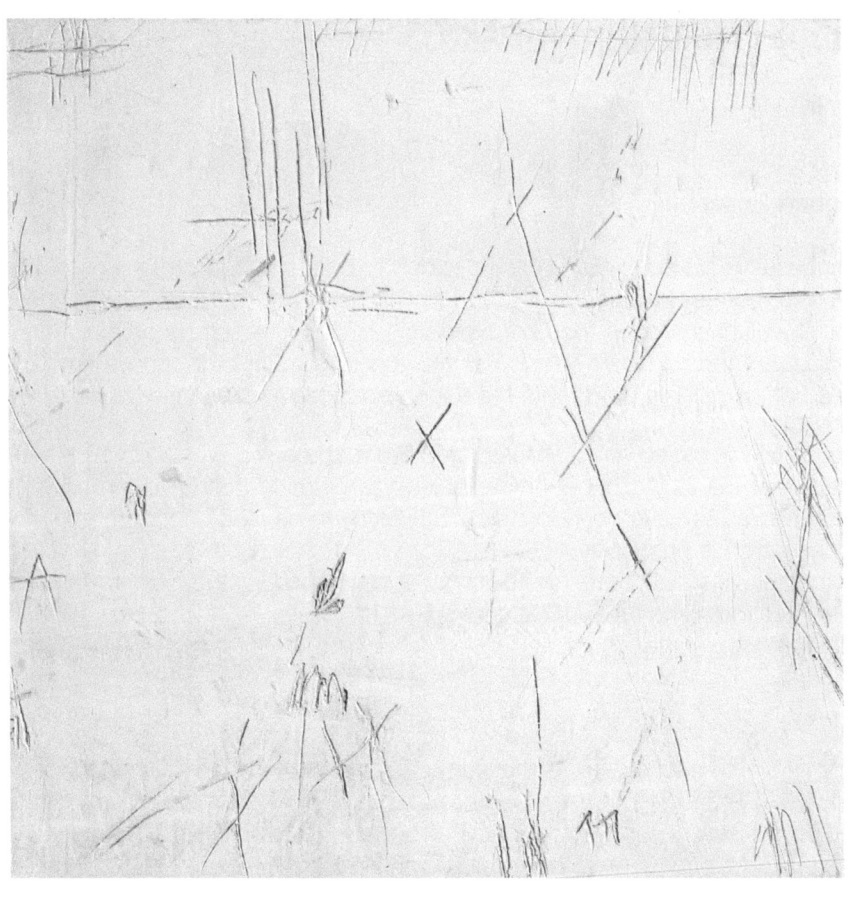

Oil and wax on aluminium. 30 x 30cm
Photo by Doug Atfield

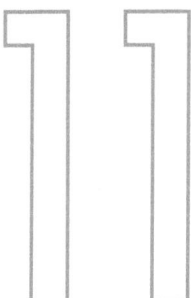

JESUS IS NAILED TO THE CROSS

Robert Priseman

For *Jesus is Nailed to the Cross* I decided to create a cruciform image of two nails to more or less actual size and similar in kind to those believed to have crucified Christ. These nails are typically 12.5 cm long, made of iron, with a gradually tapering shaft of 9mm at the top to a point of around 2mm. The head of the nail is a dome with the edges extended in the shape of a bell.

The model is based on a reconstructed nail made by Fr. Weyland which is on display at the Holy Chapel of Gerusalemme. This in turn is patterned on a nail believed to have been found by St Helena in her search for the one true cross which is on display at the Basilica of S. Croce. Both are very similar in characteristics and measurements to a nail found in the heal bone of a crucified man from A.D. 7 at the Giv'at ha Mivtar excavation of 1968 in Jerusalem.

Robert's work is held in art museums around the world, including those of The V&A, The Museum der Moderne Salzburg, The Art Gallery of New South Wales, Musée de Louvain la Neuve, The Allen Memorial Art Museum, The Mead Art Museum, The Royal Collection Windsor, The Honolulu Museum of Art and The National Galleries of Scotland.

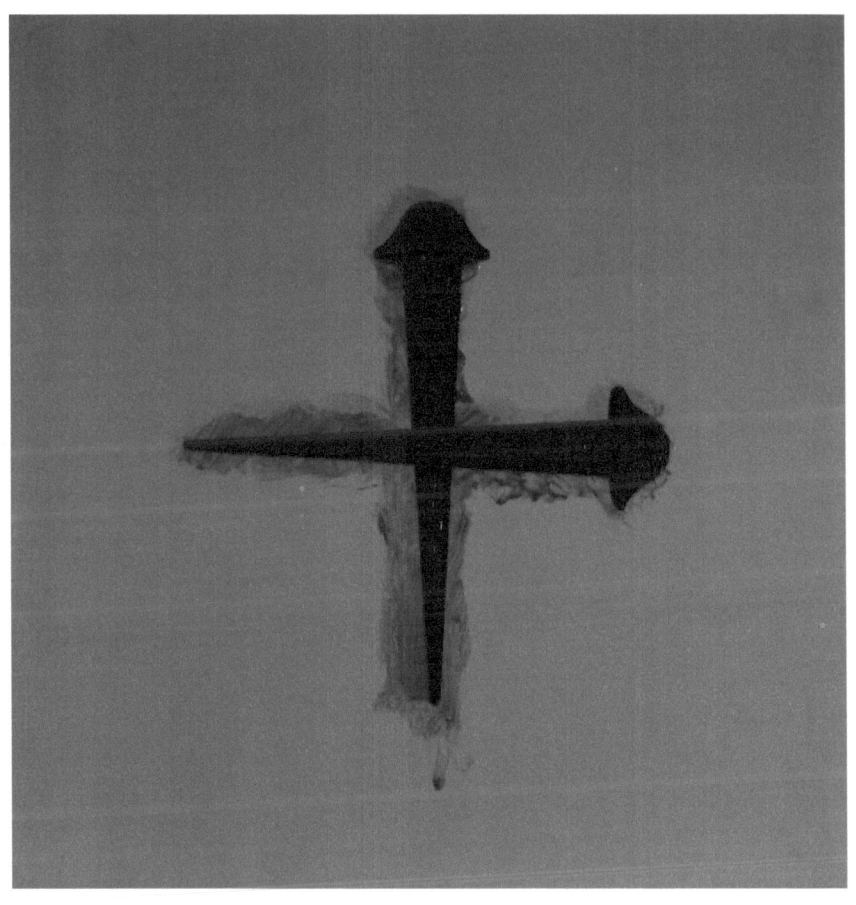

Oil on aluminium. 30 x 30cm

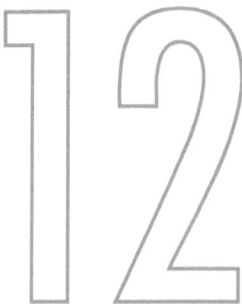

JESUS DIES ON THE CROSS

Marguerite Horner

This painting was inspired by an experience I had in Venice many years ago when I was going through a particularly difficult time, and so in a state of near desperation I went into a church and prayed for help, I wanted to be taken out of my situation, to be saved from it...I was laying the burden of my suffering at the foot of the cross, hence the fiery red flowers.

There is an earlier version of this painting and the title I gave it was 'Take me out of here into there'. I like to think that in this painting the reality of the cross appears in sharp contrast to the ephemeral nature of the passing material world surrounding it.

2014   *The OPEN WEST,* The Wilson Gallery, Cheltenham
2014   *The National Open Exhibition,* Somerset House, London
2014   *In the City,* Lion & Lamb, London
2014   *Contemporary British Painting,* Huddersfield art Gallery
2014   *ING Discerning Eye,* The Mall Galleries, London
2014   *@PaintBritain,* Ipswich Art School Gallery

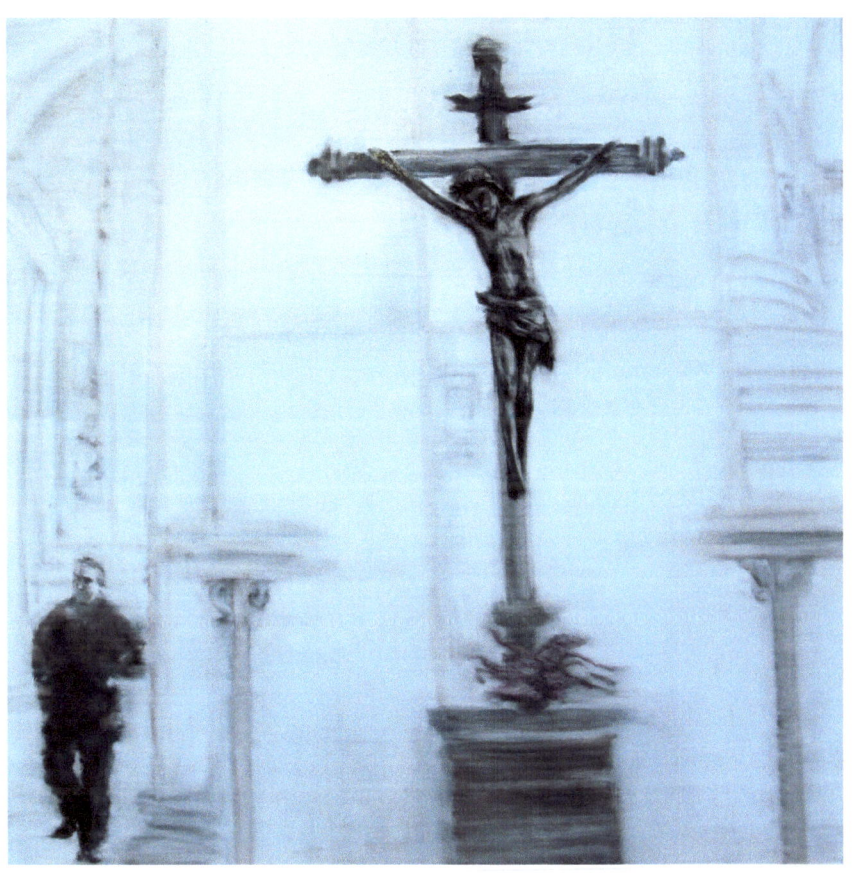

Oil on aluminium. 30 x 30cm

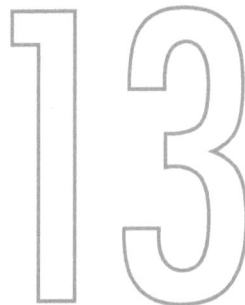

JESUS IS TAKEN DOWN FROM THE CROSS

Susan Gunn

In Scared Geometry the circle is the shape traditionally assigned to the heavens and the square to earth. In this painting, *Crucem, Sacro Terra* 2015, heaven & earth, spirit and matter are combined. The equilateral triangle references the Trinity and god's Omniscience, Omnipresence and Omnipotence.

Susan works in a contemporary way with natural earth pigments and a traditional binder that references the use of gesso used by the old masters during the Renaissance and before. The surface of the painting is allowed to dry whilst cracks and fissures appear due to environmental conditions in the studio. Each painting is unique and often divided geometrically using and sometimes subverting, the idea of the Golden section. The reference to proportion and balance also alludes to Leonardo Da Vinci's Vitruvian Man; and God being the ultimate architect and creator of the universe.

The broken surface in the painting is a metaphor for man's imperfection, the Cross, a symbol of God's love and sacrifice.

Susan received international recognition when she was awarded the Sovereign European Art Prize. She has held solo exhibitions at Norwich Castle Museum & Art Gallery, The Gallery at Norwich University of the Arts; and The Crypt, Marylebone, London. She was an inaugural member of Contemporary British Painting founded by Robert Priseman and has works in public and private collections around the world.

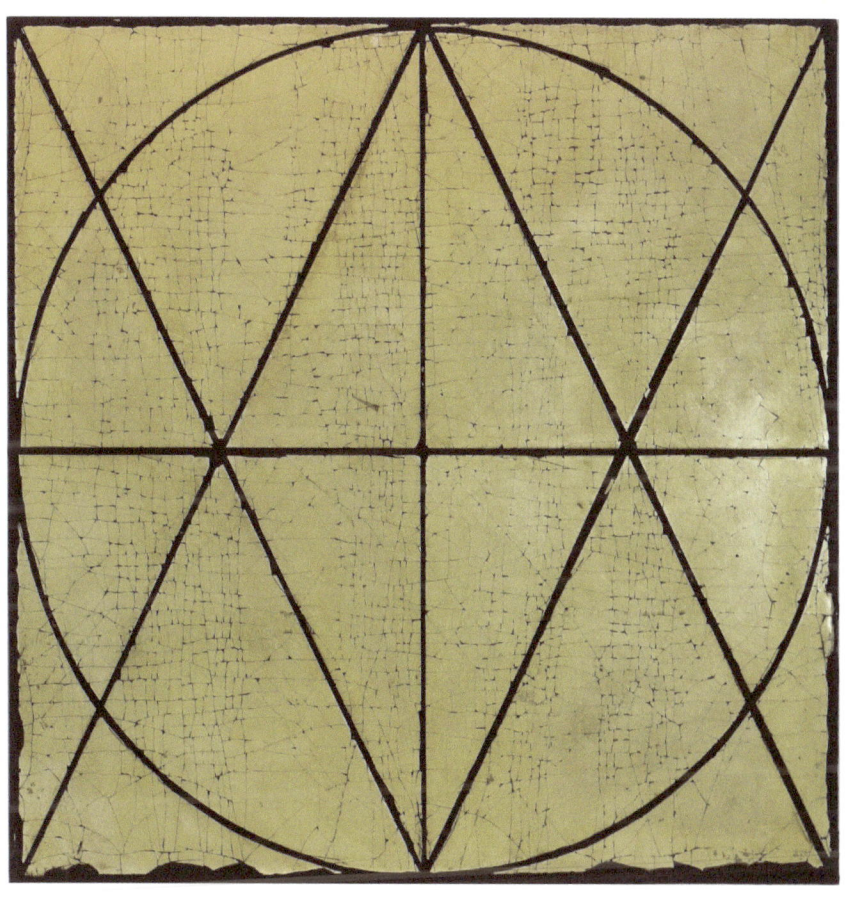

Oil, natural earth pigment, wax & gesso on canvas & aluminium. 30 x 30cm

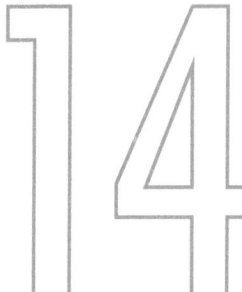

JESUS IS LAID IN THE TOMB

Alex Hanna

The painting 'Empty Pill Packs" forms part of a project which utilises everyday and overlooked objects. These objects are perceived within ambiguous surroundings and a reductionist colour/tone scheme. To some extent it asks us to remove our worldly vision - the eyes enslavement to the world's concept of what is of value and see things differently. Rather than rely upon a passive sense of vision where the eye is drawn in many directions quickly, following multiple and seductive pathways it attempts to refocus vision through a meditation with the visual.

2014	*Contemporary British Painting,* Huddersfield Art Gallery
2014	*ING Discerning Eye,* Mall Galleries, London
2014	*@PaintBritain,* Ipswich Art School Gallery
2013	*Marmite Prize,* Tannery Arts Bermondsey
2013	Royal Academy Summer Exhibition
2013	*Burning Bright* at the Hyatt Hotel London

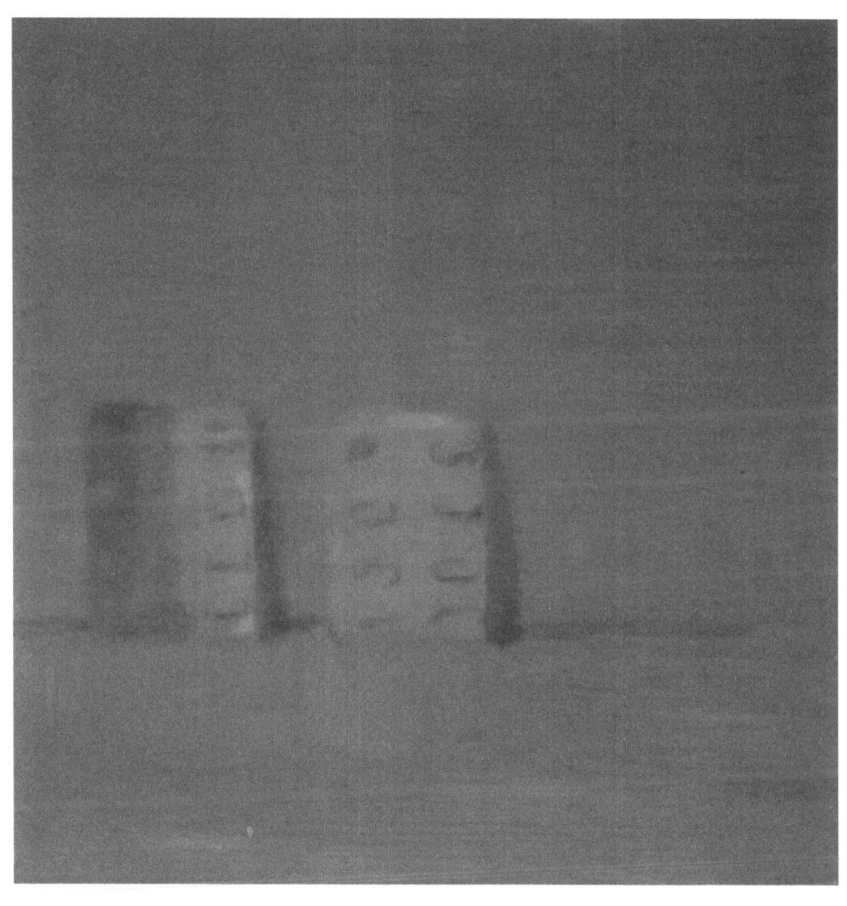

Oil on aluminium. 30 x 30cm

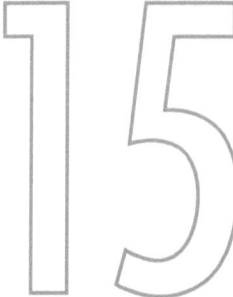

JESUS RISES FROM THE DEAD

Simon Carter

Some of the things I was thinking about while making this painting: The passage at the end of John's Gospel where the disciples are on the lake fishing and see the risen Jesus on the shore but do not recognise him; *On the Road to Tarascon,* a drawing and lost painting by Van Gogh showing himself loaded up with his painting gear and Francis Bacon's variations on it; a series of paintings I made in 2012 of a single figure in front of the sea with a distant boat; my dad on the beach wearing his sunhat.

The risen Jesus is encountered unrecognised and in unlikely places.

2014   *Contemporary British Painting,* Huddersfield Art Gallery
2014   *@PaintBritain,* Ipswich Art School Gallery
2014   *A Walk in the Park,* Art Exchange, University of Essex
2014   *Action: Abstract Painting,* Swindon Museum and Art Gallery
2013   *The Shapes of Light,* Messum's, London
2012   *Bacon to Rego,* Abbot Hall, Kendal

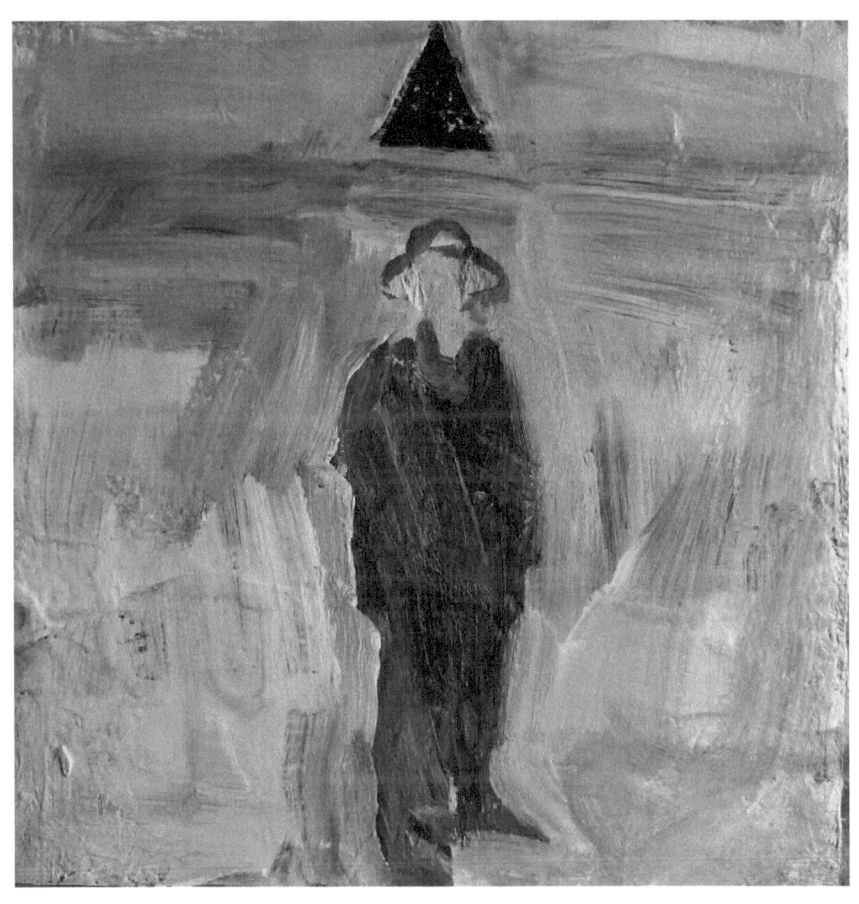

Acrylic on aluminium. 30 x 30cm

With special thanks to

Fr. Martin Boland
Noah Carter
Robert Priseman
and all the artists involved

ContemporaryBritishPainting.com

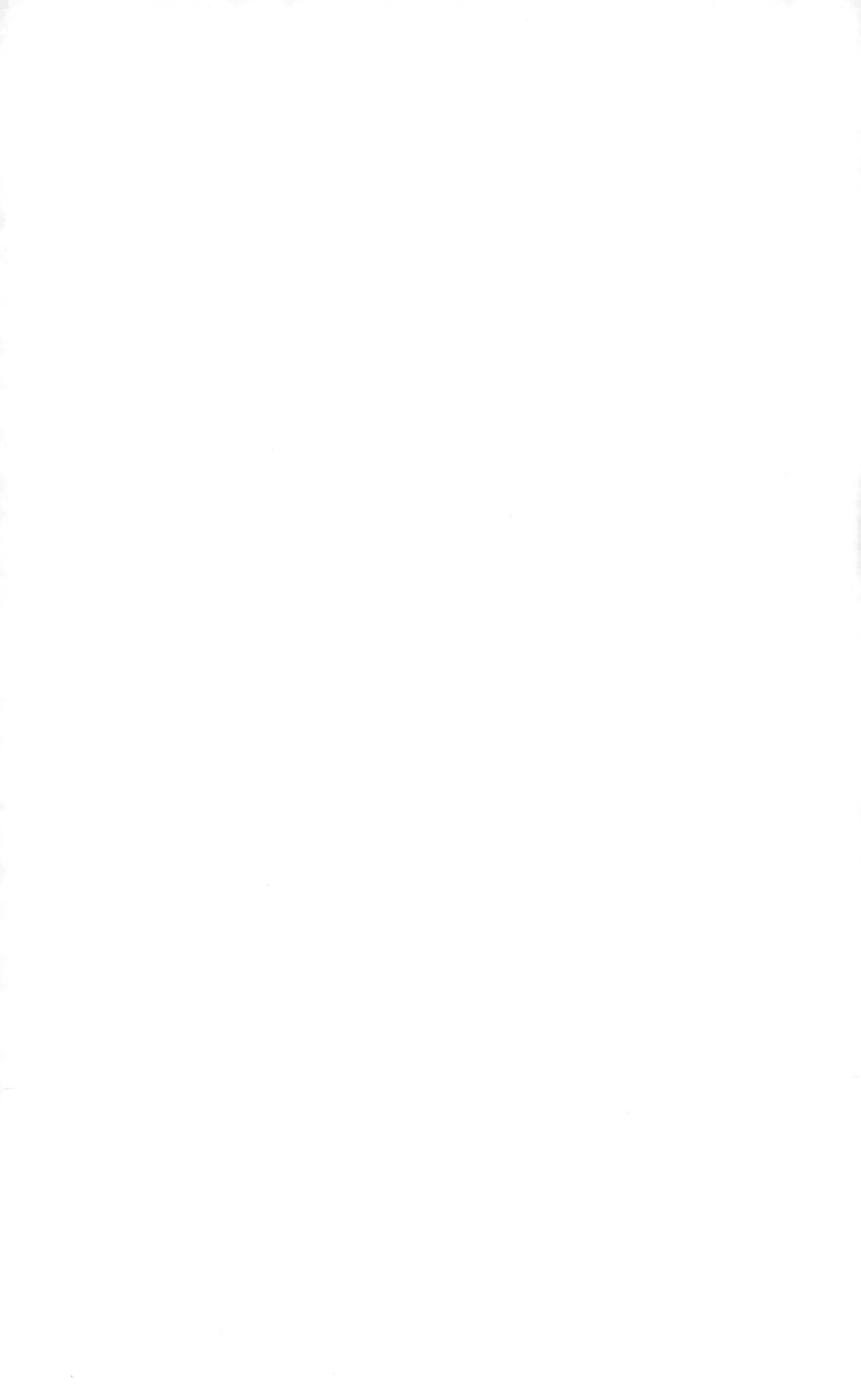

www.ingramcontent.com/pod-product-compliance
Lightning Source LLC
Chambersburg PA
CBHW040816200526
45159CB00024B/3001